ONE DIRECTION

THE OFFICIAL ANNUAL 2014

General edition ISBN: 978-0-00-752100-5
Exclusive cover edition (International) ISBN: 978-0-00-753200-1

1 3 5 7 9 10 8 6 4 2

First published in Great Britain by HarperCollins *Children's Books* in 2013

© 1 D Media Limited, 2013

All internal and back cover photography © Calvin Aurand, with the following exceptions:
pp. 4, 6-7, 12-13, 16 (bottom), 18-19, 21, 23, 25, 31, 32 (left), 33 (bottom right),
34-35, 36 (top left), 38-39, 40 (top left), 46-47, 52-53, back cover (Niall) © Myrna Suarez / Twin B Photography
pp. 56-57 © Will Bloomfield. Album cover image on pages 40, 52-53 © John Urbano.

One Direction's official photographer is Calvin Aurand. He is a music industry executive turned live music filmmaker and photographer. For the past 18 months he has toured with One Direction, using his unique perspective and behind-the-scenes access to document the band's travels around the globe. For more information visit www.krop.com/calvinaurand.

Special thanks to Jen Kelly, Targa Sahyoun, Luis Pelayo @ L2 Digital, and Ben Gonzalez

All other non-band images used under licence from Shutterstock

Front cover photograph © Rankin

Text: Sarah Delmege
Additional material: Gemma Barder
Editorial director: Neil Dunnicliffe
Design: Wayne Redwood
Cover design: James Stevens
Production: Sian Smith

With thanks to Jordan Paramor

Modest

HarperCollins *Children's Books*

CONTENTS

ON TOP OF THE WORLD

ONE Direction are the hottest band on the planet. Ever since these five lads exploded on to the scene in 2010, they have blasted the cobwebs off the pop world. The whole globe knows exactly who One Direction are. Niall Horan, Zayn Malik, Liam Payne, Harry Styles and Louis Tomlinson are, without doubt, the biggest thing to hit the music business for decades. In just three short years, they've done what even legendary bands like The Beatles and The Rolling Stones never did; two albums straight in at number one in the US plus amazing sales around the globe. No band has ever cracked the world in such a short amount of time. With that kind of success behind them, it would be easy for the guys to stand still or get complacent, but they are determined to carry on growing, both artistically and personally. "We want our music to grow with us," says Zayn. With the incredible talent, drive and strength of character that One Direction have shown so far, there's no doubt that the sky's the limit, and their story has still only just begun…

GOING THE DISTANCE

Sometimes it's easy to forget just how far One Direction have come...

T'S hard to believe, but at the beginning of 2010, the lads of One Direction didn't even know each other. Niall, Zayn, Harry, Liam and Louis all auditioned separately for the seventh season of *The X Factor*. Inspiration struck judges Simon Cowell and Nicole Scherzinger, who put the five guys into a band and the story began. Since then, One Direction have ushered in a new era of pop. Their *Up All Night* album stormed charts all over the world, and they were the first UK act to open at No.1 in the US Billboard charts with their debut album. One Direction-mania had begun.

Their second album, *Take Me Home*, was one of the most hotly anticipated releases ever. Questions buzzed around the guys. Would it, could it, be as good as their first? There was a pretty obvious answer. No group was going to have such a large impact and then simply disappear. Sure enough, the album was a smash hit the world over. As Niall says, "When you make the second album, I think the thing to do is to outdo your first album. Personally, I think we've done that."

ONE DIRECTION

"WHEN YOU MAKE THE SECOND ALBUM, I THINK THE THING TO DO IS TO OUTDO YOUR FIRST ALBUM. PERSONALLY, I THINK WE'VE DONE THAT."
— NIALL

They certainly had. The lads have every reason to be proud of the album. It took the band to the top of the charts and to new heights all over the world. In fact, hearing that One Direction have broken a music record is starting to feel like déjà vu! They've sold out worldwide tours, have over 45 million followers on Twitter, played at the 2012 Olympics Games Closing Ceremony, won countless awards and even hold a Guinness World Record.

Still, none of the band expected this to happen, or realised just how big One Direction would become. They've achieved so much in a short period of time and they're very grateful to everyone who's helped them along the way. "We have an incredible team of people around us who have helped us achieve this," says Liam.

And of course, the guys haven't forgotten the most important people who got them here. "We just want to say a massive thanks to all the fans who supported us," says Harry. "We can send tweets and thank them, but 140 characters is never going to be enough to say how much it means."

The lads sit down for a well-earned break and a good old gossip!

EXCLUSIVE INTERVIEW!

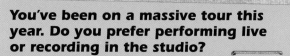

You've been on a massive tour this year. Do you prefer performing live or recording in the studio?

HARRY: I prefer touring because it's more fun. We all get to hang out with each other loads and we get to see the fans!

LIAM: Both, actually. They're both the best parts of the job. Probably a bit more of the recording side, now. We've been working on the third album and Louis and I have written a song that feels really good. I love the creative process.

NIALL: Touring, definitely. I do like both, but I like the routine of touring and the fact that all you have to worry about is the show.

LOUIS: Recording is really, really fun, but the nice thing about touring is that you have a bit of a routine. We have more of a schedule to stick to.

ZAYN: I love recording, simply because it's quite chilled out and we get to be creative. But touring is amazing as well, so it's hard to pick one. Can I have both?

Which song do you most like to perform?

LIAM: I really enjoy *C'mon, C'mon*, because the crowd love it and they always sing it back to us.

LOUIS: *Loved You First*.

HARRY: I really enjoy performing *Kiss You*, *She's Not Afraid* and *Little Things*. We never get bored of any songs when we are on tour, because we are able to mix things up each evening.

NIALL: On the *Take Me Home* tour it was *Heart Attack* and *C'mon, C'mon*.

ZAYN: *Tell Me a Lie* and *More Than This* are both good to sing on stage.

DATE OF EVENT.

25.06.13

ONE DIRECTION

"I REALLY ENJOY PERFORMING *KISS YOU*, *SHE'S NOT AFRAID* AND *LITTLE THINGS*." – HARRY

What was it like making your first movie, *This Is Us*?

ZAYN: Amazing and weird at the same time. It was strange having the cameras on us all of the time, but we did end up forgetting about them.

HARRY: We never imagined we'd be making a movie, so it was pretty surreal, but we had a really good laugh doing it. We've seen ourselves on TV many times, but being up on a cinema screen is totally different.

LIAM: It was good. The whole time we were making it, we were looking forward to seeing the final product. We really enjoyed seeing it coming together, and it's something really personal we could share with everyone.

NIALL: It was weird because the cameras were with us every step of the way, but it was good fun.

LOUIS: Making the movie was amazing. We never thought we would be doing something like that, but it felt similar to *The X Factor* because we had cameras following us everywhere back then, too. It was pretty chilled out.

Who is your favourite actor and why do you think they are so great?

HARRY: Johnny Depp is an incredible actor. He can play any role, no matter how weird, and totally pull it off.

LOUIS: I love Leonardo DiCaprio and I always have done. He's a sick actor.

NIALL: Robert De Niro. He can play any kind of character and be amazing. He's an all-rounder.

ZAYN: Al Pacino, because he's a great method actor and he chooses really good roles.

LIAM: Johnny Depp, because he's Captain Jack Sparrow, who is the coolest character ever.

"Making the movie was amazing. We never thought we would be doing something like that, but it felt similar to The X Factor because we had cameras following us everywhere back then, too. It was pretty chilled out." – Louis

Which leading lady would you like to act with?

LIAM: Emma Watson, because she's very cute.

HARRY: Jennifer Lawrence. She's gorgeous, but she also seems really down to earth and like she'd be a good laugh.

LOUIS: Natalie Portman, because she's phenomenal.

NIALL: Anne Hathaway. She's gorgeous.

ZAYN: Scarlett Johansson is amazing.

If you could be any other famous person for 24 hours, who would it be?

LOUIS: Someone like James Morrison, because he's got a sick voice.

HARRY: Russell Brand, because I find him really interesting.

NIALL: Channing Tatum or Ryan Reynolds, because the girls fall at their feet!

ZAYN: Kanye West.

LIAM: Jennifer Aniston. She's so hot. I saw her on an advert the other day and she still looks amazing.

If you could be transported into any video game, which one would it be?

HARRY: *FIFA*. Every time. I'd love to be an expert footballer.

LIAM: *Call of Duty*, although that could really hurt.

LOUIS: I'd say *FIFA*, too, so I could get really good at football.

NIALL: Yeah, it would have to be *FIFA*, because I'd love to be a good footballer, too.

ZAYN: *Resident Evil*, because, even though it sounds weird, I've always wondered what it would be like if zombies took over the world. I'd love to get the chance to shoot some zombies!

Which sport are you best at?

HARRY: Badminton, but I don't get to play it very much.
LIAM: Boxing, because I used to do it when I was young.
LOUIS: Football, definitely.
ZAYN: Cricket. I played it a lot at school.
NIALL: Football, but I would like to be better.

Which sporting star do you most admire?

HARRY: Usain Bolt. I thought the Olympics were amazing generally, but watching him was a real highlight.
LIAM: Thierry Henry. It's the va va voom!
LOUIS: David Beckham, because he's cool and so talented.
NIALL: Lionel Messi. A lot of people say you can't make it as a footballer if you're small, but he's proved them wrong. He's only about 5' 7" and he's the best player in the world.
ZAYN: David Beckham, because he seems like a nice bloke and he's an amazing footballer.

What's the scariest thing you've ever done?

LIAM: Probably jumping off a building in New Zealand. But, to be honest, I was more excited than scared.
HARRY: When we were fishing in San Diego, Liam caught a baby shark. He threw it back in the water, then I jumped in for a swim afterwards. It seemed like a good idea at the time!
NIALL: Being on the flying platform on our tour. If you were to fall off it, you'd be in serious trouble. I was scared of that to begin with, but I did get used to it.
ZAYN: The boys forced me to go on a rollercoaster ride at Universal Studios and I hate things like that. It was called *The Incredible Hulk* and it was awful. I won't ever do it again. Rollercoasters give me headaches.
LOUIS: Auditioning for *The X Factor*. I was absolutely terrified.

What was the cheekiest thing you did at school?

LIAM: I once climbed on the roof to fetch a ball, and I also put a daddy longlegs in a girl's bag!
LOUIS: I flashed my bum when I was in *Grease*. I got very told off. I was never a great student, but I wasn't that badly behaved.
NIALL: I was always late for school – I like my sleep too much.
ZAYN: I got excluded for four days. I wasn't allowed to go on our school trip as a result and I was gutted.
HARRY: I once took a sandwich from the canteen without paying. I got caught and got properly told off. I didn't do it again.

"WHEN WE WERE FISHING IN SAN DIEGO, LIAM CAUGHT A BABY SHARK. HE THREW IT BACK IN THE WATER, THEN I JUMPED IN FOR A SWIM AFTERWARDS. IT SEEMED LIKE A GOOD IDEA AT THE TIME!" – HARRY

1D

1D RULE

If you could travel back in time to any decade, which one would you choose?

HARRY: The 60s, because the music was cool and it seemed like a fun time to be around.

LIAM: I'd go back to when dinosaurs were alive, so I could check them all out.

LOUIS: The 70s, because it looks cool. They wore bad clothes, but no one cared.

NIALL: The 50s, because I love the whole Rat Pack era. My whole house is covered in posters of Frank Sinatra.

ZAYN: The 60s, because it looked cool and very laid back.

Tell us a secret!

LIAM: I'm more of a perfectionist than I realise. I can't share drinks bottles and I'm not a fan of Louis nicking my Perinaise sauce!

LOUIS: I'm going to get loads more tattoos to add to my random collection.

NIALL: I don't know if anyone's noticed, but although I'm left-handed, I play the guitar right-handed. I also play golf and eat right-handed.

ZAYN: I've got six toes. I don't really, but let's start the rumour... A proper secret is that I've got a tattoo on my leg. It's a crisscross symbol.

HARRY: I almost cried when we won a Brit Award. I was genuinely close to tears.

INSIDE THE LIFE OF 1D

They might be global superstars but Harry, Zayn, Louis, Liam and Niall are still just regular lads...

THE lads have been busy reflecting on what they have achieved so quickly in their career. "I don't think it will ever sink in," laughs Niall. Despite their whirlwind success, the guys have somehow managed to keep their egos firmly in check. With such huge fame, it would be so easy for their heads to become inflated. But everyone who comes into contact with the band is instantly overwhelmed by their sense of fun and down-to-earth honesty. It's clear that no matter what life-changing adventures being in One Direction brings, the guys will always have smiles on their faces and a complete lack of attitude. As Niall says, "What we do isn't normal, but we are."

Louis agrees with him, "We're just ourselves – cheeky, immature and quirky."

"As a band we are quite chilled out people," explains Liam. "We don't take ourselves too seriously and that's important in surviving the showbiz world."

They might be five of the most recognisable faces on the planet right now, but when they're not working, all of the band make sure they find time to kick back and chill out; to live as ordinary a life as possible. "We do the same things every lad our age does," says Harry. "We go out, we have fun, we meet girls and stuff like that."

All five guys like nothing better than having the time to do regular stuff like hitting the gym, shopping for clothes, playing *FIFA*, slobbing out in front of the TV, or just having fun with friends.

There's no doubt that it's the friendship between the lads that helps to keep them so grounded. Despite the amount of time they spend together, the guys have never had a serious falling out. "People still ask whether we really get on or not, and we genuinely do," laughs Liam. "We're the brothers we never had."

"WE DON'T TAKE OURSELVES TOO SERIOUSLY AND THAT'S IMPORTANT IN SURVIVING THE SHOWBIZ WORLD." – LIAM

GET CLOSE TO HARRY

BIRTHDATE:
1 February 1994

ZODIAC SIGN:
Aquarius

PERSONALITY:
Aquarian guys are outgoing and love talking to new people. They're friends with everyone. However, they have a shy side, especially around crushes.

- Harry's style is the perfect mix of dressed up and dressed down. He really knows how to work a T-shirt and a blazer.

- Harry says he never gets tired of hugging 1D fans or the other guys in the band!

- His curls are always so perfect you'd think it must take him hours to style. "It actually doesn't take that long," he laughs.

A FIRST DATE WITH HARRY!   ★ EXCLUSIVE ★

What three things do you look for in a girl?
A nice smile, nice eyes and someone who makes me laugh. Being able to have a laugh together is really important.

What would you wear on a first date?
Black skinny jeans, boots and a shirt. Pretty much what I wear most days anyway. If it's a first date it should be pretty relaxed.

What's your perfect first date destination?
Going out for dinner is always nice because you get a chance to talk properly to each other.

Phone on or off?
I'd have it on, but I wouldn't look at it to see if anyone's called or phoned me until after the date had finished.

Harry Styles

GET CLOSE TO NIALL

RTHDATE:
September 1993

DIAC SIGN:
go

RSONALITY:
gos are thoughtful and sincere.
ey like staying in more than going
t, and friends and family are the
ost important people to them.

- Niall was born to be a performer. He even played Oliver in the school musical when he was 10!

- Despite being so successful, Niall still gets a bit nervous before going on stage.

- The rest of the lads feel most protective of Niall. "Even though he isn't the youngest, he's the one we feel most maternal towards," says Zayn. Awww.

★ EXCLUSIVE ★ 1D

A FIRST DATE WITH NIALL!

What three things do you look for in a girl?
A nice smile, a good sense of humour and I like girls who can play instruments. I think it's cool if a girl can play guitar.

What would you wear on a first date?
I'd rock up in a pair of jeans.

What's your perfect first date destination?
The Six Flags theme park in California. It's amazing.

Phone on or off?
On silent. That's a good compromise.

NIALL HORAN

GET CLOSE TO ZAYN

BIRTHDATE:
12 January 1993

ZODIAC SIGN:
Capricorn

PERSONALITY:
Capricorns are emotional, so Zayn does get upset sometimes. But he's a total sweetie too.

- Zayn is very artistic. "What I love about drawing," he says, "is it allows you to take some time out and express yourself without having to say too much."

- Zayn is always late. "I like my sleep, so I make the guys late a lot," he admits.

- Zayn loves how the band are growing up. "We're getting older and so is our music. But not too drastically!"

★ EXCLUSIVE ★

A FIRST DATE WITH ZAYN!

What three things do you look for in a girl?
A good sense of humour, someone who looks after themself, and nice teeth.

What would you wear on a first date?
Something smart. Maybe a shirt, jeans and shoes.

What's your perfect first date destination?
I'm pretty old school, so cinema and dinner. Bowling is good, because it's a laugh and a good icebreaker.

Phone on or off?
Off for a first date. I'm not bothered about my phone anyway, and you're supposed to be on a nice date!

What would you talk about?
General interests like books and films. You don't want to get into anything heavy on a first date.

Zayn Malik

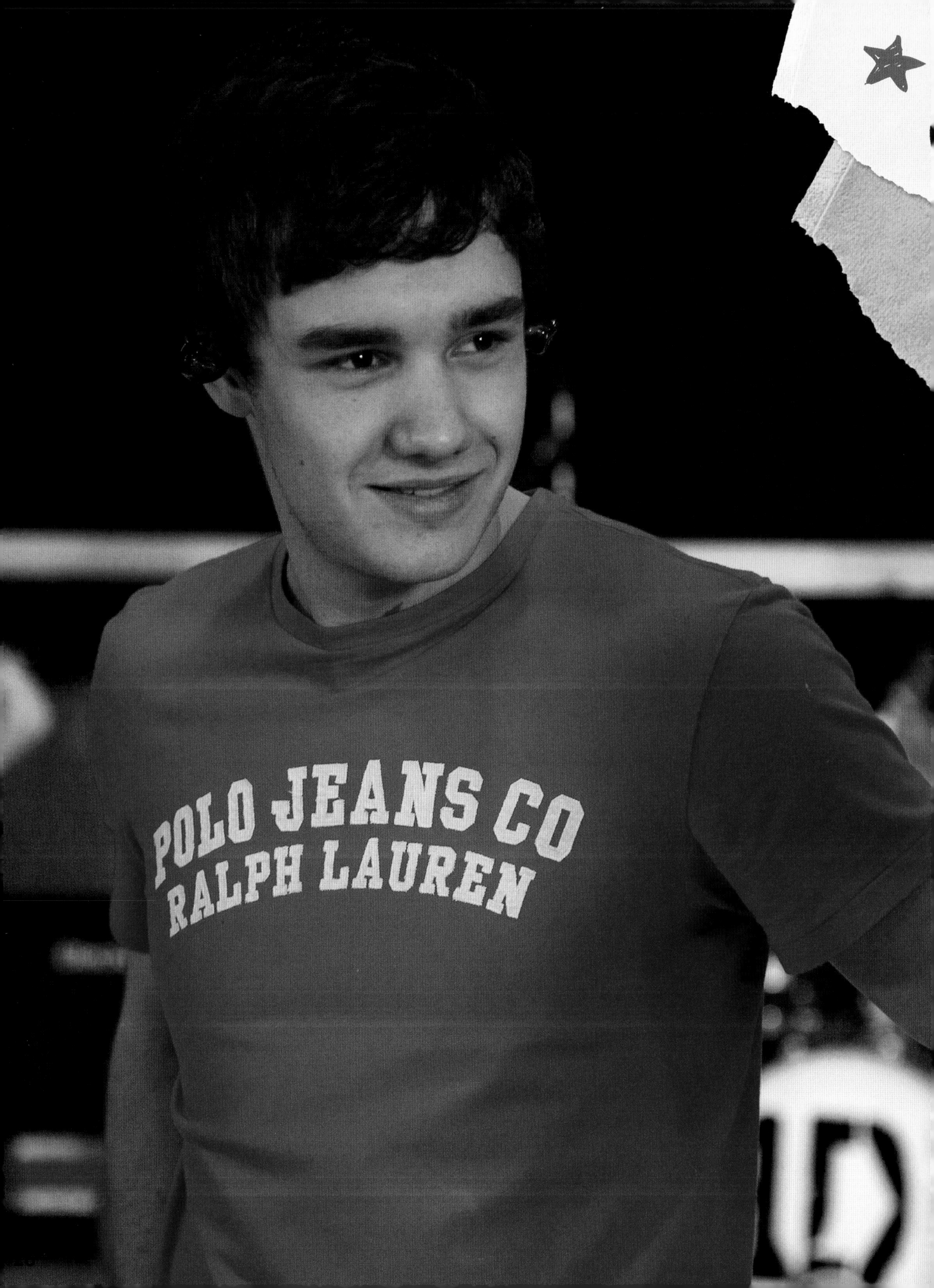
POLO JEANS CO
RALPH LAUREN

GET CLOSE TO LIAM

BIRTHDATE:
29 August 1993

ZODIAC SIGN:
Virgo

PERSONALITY:
Virgos like Liam are sweet. They can get a bit shy in front of large groups of people. They'd rather spend time one on one than be at a huge party.

- He reckons he's the band's best dancer. "I definitely have the best dance moves," he grins. "I'm the king of the dance floor."

- Liam reckons spending time with Niall is rubbing off on him. "Sometimes I do an Irish accent without noticing."

LIAM PAYNE

★ EXCLUSIVE ★

A FIRST DATE WITH LIAM!

What three things do you look for in a girl?
Someone who isn't too 'in your face'; I like girls who are a bit shy on a first date.

What would you wear on a first date?
Probably just a T-shirt, some skinny jeans and Converse.

What's your perfect first date destination?
I think it would be nice to go out on a boat. Somewhere like San Diego, because it's a beautiful place.

Phone on or off?
Off, definitely.

What would you talk about?
Anything that springs to mind. We could do some fun things and go swimming.

27

GET CLOSE TO LOUIS

BIRTHDATE:
24 December 1991

ZODIAC SIGN:
Capricorn

PERSONALITY:
Capricorn guys love to be around big groups of people. They are always the life of any party! Like most Capricorns, Louis is a daydreamer.

- He can't dance. "When I dance, it's always a joke," he says.

- Louis is always joking around with the other members of the band or playing pranks on them.

- Louis is very close to his mum and sisters and he's done tons of charity work with children.

★ EXCLUSIVE ★

A FIRST DATE WITH LOUIS!

What three things do you look for in a girl?
A girl who does her own thing. I like someone with a good sense of humour, and someone who laughs at my jokes.

What would you wear on a first date?
A decent T-shirt and some skinny jeans. Nothing too fancy.

What's your perfect first date destination?
The cinema and a meal are standard. You can't go wrong.

Phone on or off?
It should be off, but it would be on. I often get told off for having my phone on all of the time.

What would you talk about?
I'd probably try and break the ice and tell a few jokes. I always find it important to ask people about themselves, so I'd have some questions ready.

1D IN 3D

It was the moment that every 1D fan in the world was waiting for: *One Direction: This Is Us.* A front row seat to watch the lads' lives – in 3D. The band knew how excited their fans would be about the film, and from the moment making a movie had first been mentioned, the guys knew they had to give it everything. After all, lots of other superstars have released their own concert movies, so the lads knew they had to do something really special. They decided they wanted to reveal One Direction in full and show the fans exactly what they are about. As Niall says, "The fans know us, but we want them to know us a little deeper."

First they had to find the right director. The guys knew they had to find someone with the right chemistry, that they felt comfortable around. Oscar-nominated film-maker Morgan Spurlock has been in the business for years. He's a critically-acclaimed director, well-versed in making documentaries and, more importantly, the band liked him straight away. "We just clicked," says Liam.

Morgan and his film crew travelled everywhere with the band, from the moment they woke up in the morning until they were tucked up in bed. "They've actually been in the toilet with us," laughs Niall. "No lie."

Although the pressure was on, the guys had fun recording. Yes, it was a serious business, requiring long hours of work, but they loved every minute of it. "It's going to be amazing to look on it in years to come and just be like, 'This is when I was a lad,'" says Louis.

Liam agrees, "You know what we always say, when we left home to do *The X Factor* our parents were like, 'Make sure you take loads of pictures,' but we've got a film to do that for us now so we can be lazy."

The band are rightly proud of the film. What emerges from the movie is a picture of a band who work tirelessly at their craft; are true entertainers and talented singers who absolutely adore their fans. They are having the time of their lives, living their dream and they want to inspire others to know they can achieve great things too.

Everyone who has watched it can't help but see what the fans have known all along; that these are five charming guys, who haven't let the overwhelming events of the last few years go to their heads. By the time the credits roll, the lads have proved yet again that the buzz surrounding One Direction is no hype. The movie shows just how much they deserve their success.

They are genuinely talented, have truly great voices and, although they like to have a laugh and enjoy themselves, they have an incredibly professional approach to their work and are hungry for success. As Liam says, "We didn't know what lay ahead when we started out – the late nights, the early mornings, travelling, never seeing your family and friends. But we wouldn't change it for the world."

Despite the toughness of touring, the film shows that the guys are overjoyed to be doing their jobs and give being in One Direction everything they have.

"THE FANS KNOW US, BUT WE WANT THEM TO KNOW US A LITTLE DEEPER."
– NIALL

THE BEST MOVIE IN HISTORY... EVER

One Direction: This Is Us.

ON-SET SECRETS!

WHAT'S THE SILLIEST THING THAT HAPPENED DURING FILMING?

Zayn: Louis did a lot of funny things. But then Louis always does a lot of funny things. I don't want to give anything away, but it's worth watching the movie just to see what he gets up to.

Liam: We were filming an interview in Japan and we had a translator, and we kept imagining what was really being said that we couldn't understand. That was a good laugh!

Niall: We do stupid stuff all of the time and we're always having a laugh so people will get to see just how ridiculous we can be. There are some funny, unexpected moments.

Louis: We do stupid, random things every day and they've all been captured.

JULY 2010

One Direction officially form on *The X Factor* UK. Zayn, Harry, Louis, Niall and Liam all audition separately, but judges Simon Cowell and Nicole Scherzinger suggest they form a band. Brilliant idea, guys!

DECEMBER 2010

Even though the guys end up third on *The X Factor*, it works out for them in the end. Shortly after leaving the show, Simon Cowell signs One Direction to his record label.

SEPTEMBER 2011

One Direction's first single, *What Makes You Beautiful*, debuts at number one on the UK singles chart. Suddenly everyone knows who they are!

NOVEMBER 2011

1D's number one debut in the UK catches the attention of Columbia Records in the US and the label signs the guys. A total British invasion takes over the States.

Up All Night, 1D's debut album, is released in the UK and Ireland.

MARCH 2012

Over 15,000 fans flood the streets outside the *Today* show in New York City to watch One Direction perform.

Girls all over the country are so excited about the guys' performance that 'TODAY' starts trending on Twitter.

MARCH 2012

Up All Night is released in the US and immediately debuts at number one on the US charts. Shortly after, the guys embark on their first worldwide headlining tour.

AUGUST 2012

The Olympics have plenty of memorable moments, but One Direction get more buzz than anyone when they perform at the Olympic Games Closing Ceremony, playing *What Makes You Beautiful.*

SEPTEMBER 2012

To nobody's surprise, One Direction totally kill it at the MTV Music Awards, winning Best New Artist, Best Pop Video, and Most Share-worthy Video. Then they dominate the stage with a performance of *One Thing.*

The *Live While We're Young* music video is released and gets 8.24 million views in the first 24 hours, breaking a record previously held by Justin Bieber. Then it becomes the most pre-ordered single EVER in Sony Music history.

FEBRUARY 2013

The lads become the first winners of an award recognising global success at the BRITS. They perform their charity single, *One Way or Another,* which tops the charts in more than 60 countries.

2013 WORLD TOUR

The guys kick off their world tour in style with a massive London show at the O2 Arena. After the event Louis tweeted: "Loved it !!!!"

PLUS An amazing stadium tour has been announced for 2014!

And... there are too many other exciting moments to mention! We're sure you have your favourites!

★ **EXCLUSIVE** ★

STYLE SECRETS

The 1D lads have certainly developed their own style since becoming world-famous popstars! Check out their most intimate styling secrets...

ZAYN

Zayn's style is sleek and cool with a retro vibe. Although he's almost always smart, he does like to make his look more casual with a pair of his famous Converse!

What's your favourite item of clothing?
A leather jacket I got from a charity shop.

Who is the most stylish member of the group?
Louis is quite stylish, because he takes risks and wears a lot of bright colours.

What's the worst fashion mistake you have made?
It was when we were on *The X Factor* and Simon said we could wear whatever we wanted for a group performance. We decided to be a bit stupid, so I got this gilet and painted it pink and green and wore it on live TV. It was horrible – it's in a bin somewhere!

NIALL

Niall's style is comfy, casual and cool. He likes teaming smart tees and polo shirts with cardigans or hoodies. His look matches perfectly his laid-back personality!

What's your favourite item of clothing?
My SUPRA shoes. I wear them all of the time.

Who is the most stylish member of the group?
I think there are a few, but Zayn can wear anything and it looks good on him. The other day he had his shirt wrapped around his jeans and a hoodie on and it looked sick.

What's the worst fashion mistake you have made?
I make a lot of them, but in my head it's all good. I've worn some dodgy stuff in the past. I wore a leopard print jumper with all of these colours on it that looked awful. It looked a lot better when I saw it on the website.

LOUIS
Louis likes to have fun with fashion and is never afraid of wearing something new. He looks super-cute in quirky T-shirts and really works the preppy style!

What's your favourite item of clothing?
Black skinny jeans. I wear them pretty much every day.

Who is the most stylish member of the group?
I'm going to say Harry.

What's the worst fashion mistake you have made?
I think I overdid stripes for a while. They were on-trend, but I was wearing them every day. Also, wearing shoes without socks is a cool look, but it's just stupid in the winter time!

LIAM
Liam is the master of understated cool. He likes subtle colours and laid-back style and is happiest when he's dressed in something he's picked out himself.

What's your favourite item of clothing?
This sounds really 'diva', but I've got a Dior coat that I really like. It's quite cool, but I don't get to wear it that often.

Who is the most stylish member of the group?
I'm going to say probably Harry. He looks cool and he dresses smartly.

What's the worst fashion mistake you have made?
When I cut off all my hair the first time around. I looked like Spock from Star Trek. It didn't suit me at all.

HARRY
Harry's style has gone from cute 'boy next door' to all-out smart rock god. He's made the T-shirt and blazer look his own and isn't afraid to be different. Bow ties are cool!

What's your favourite item of clothing?
My Rolling Stones T-shirt. It's cool, but also really comfortable.

Who is the most stylish member of the group?
I think we all have our moments! Zayn always looks cool.

What's the worst fashion mistake you have made?
I once wore a gilet, which in retrospect was a very bad idea. I won't be wearing one again any time in the near future.

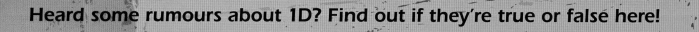

FACT OR FICTION?

Heard some rumours about 1D? Find out if they're true or false here!

Zayn loves sharks!

True: his favourite is a Hammerhead.

Liam was in *The X Factor* twice!

True! Liam auditioned in 2008 and got all the way through to the judges' houses.

Harry suffers from Ophidiophobia!

True! That's a fear of snakes to me and you.

The *Up All Night* UK tour sold out in just 13 minutes!

False. It was 12!

The boys aren't really friends!

It's true, the 1D lads aren't really friends... they're WAY closer than that! "We're like brothers," says Niall. They're always laughing and having fun together.

Harry wants to dye his hair purple!

This rumour is totally true! Harry says that if he could dye his hair any colour, it would be dark purple. "I feel that would look the most brown," he laughs.

Louis' bum is insured!

Totally false. Louis says he hasn't insured his behind, but thinks this rumour is laugh-out-loud funny! "Hilarious story," he grins. "But why? I'm not going to lose it, am I? Why insure it?"

Niall's first ever gig was Busted!

True! Niall went to see the guys when he was still at primary school.

LIFE ON THE ROAD

With their world stadium tour, the lads prove that hard work and a truly brilliant album make for one of the best shows you'll ever see, EVER.

Being the biggest band in the world means 1D have a lot to live up to, especially when it comes to touring. Although the guys had already played to thousands of fans the world over, their stadium tour felt very different – especially as many of the tour's concerts sold out a year in advance. "We were definitely nervous," says Liam. "We didn't want to let anyone down."

But fans had nothing to fear; the lads didn't let any pre-gig jitters spoil the show. Everyone who saw them couldn't help but fall in love with the band, who looked and sounded like a dream. Night after night, the stadiums were packed with screaming fans as Niall, Louis, Liam, Zayn and Harry showed that they were all truly born to perform, clearly loving every moment of being on stage. "I still can't quite believe this is my job," says Niall, "playing a concert to the best fans on the planet." Every night One Direction worked their magic, blowing the crowds away with their energy and their talent. The fans loved the songs and they loved the lads who sang them even more.

TOUR HIGHLIGHTS

- Niall strumming his electric and acoustic guitars during several songs in the second act.
- Seeing just how close the band obviously are.
- Liam handing out bear hugs.
- The 1D version of *Teenage Dirtbag*.
- The lads saying a huge heartfelt thank you to their fans at the end of each show.
- Twitter questions.
- Bouncing off each other during *One Way or Another*.
- Liam talking and talking and talking and talking and talking some more…

TOUR VIDEO BEST BITS

- Liam tidying up.
- Harry having a bath.
- Niall and Zayn dressed up as hippies, playing *WMYB* to an unsuspecting crowd.
- Harry and Liam made-up as old people who surprise strangers by suddenly breaking into a really fast run.
- Louis putting on a fat suit and offering free hugs to oblivious members of the general public.

Set List

Up All Night
I Would
Heart Attack
More Than This
Loved You First
One Thing
C'mon C'mon
Change My Mind
One Way or Another/Teenage Kicks
Last First Kiss
Moments
Back For You
Summer Love
Over Again
Little Things
Teenage Dirtbag
Rock Me
She's Not Afraid
Kiss You
Live While We're Young
What Makes You Beautiful

ONE DIRECTION

1D'S BEST TWEETS

No doubt about it, One Direction's tweets always brighten our day...

NIALL
Wohooooo sun's out again! Loving it! Shorts are on, bringing the chicken legs out!

HARRY
I feel ollllllllddddddddddd.

LOUIS
Zayn is wearing stripes!!! I feel like I've been cheated on!!

LIAM
I love the fact I grew up wanting a brother and now I have four, love u boys :)

HARRY
Sometimes I see things and think… 'I do have quite a lot of hair'

LIAM
pooooooop is all I have to say

NIALL
Up early! Don't think I went to bed early enough haha! Sunrise this mornin ! Gna be fun

LIAM
Not to alarm anyone but I genuinely think I have left my toothbrush in the last place we were in

ZAYN
Hi everyone, just a quick message to say I love all you guys, without your support I don't know what I'd do :) x

LOUIS
Gna do some writing today feeling philosophical aha ;p x

ZAYN
If the love is real, it will rise above.

1D MUSICAL INFLUENCES

From the very beginning there's been music in One Direction's lives. "We've all loved all kinds of music since we were small," says Niall. But since being in One Direction and travelling the world, a whole new avenue of music has opened up and has influenced the guys. These days, when asked which artists are getting major rotation on their personal playlists, the guys are most likely to name an R&B rapper or an indie rocker.

There's no doubt that the lads live and breathe music, and want to write more of their own material. Harry says they all write whenever they can: "On the road and stuff, we're in a lot of planes and in a lot of hotels," he says, "and obviously you just write there." It's important to the band that their music reflects them, as they continue to grow and develop artistically. "We want to believe in what we're singing," says Niall. "And we want our fans to keep loving what we're doing."

HARRY

Who are your biggest musical influences?
Definitely Chris Martin from Coldplay and Kings of Leon.

What are you listening to right now?
A band called Frightened Rabbit, who are brilliant.

What's the best gig you've ever been to?
An American group called Haim, who were absolutely amazing live.

HARRY'S PLAYLIST
Yellow – Coldplay
Swim Until You Can't See Land – Frightened Rabbit
Falling - Haim

LIAM

Who are your biggest musical influences?
I'll say Michael Bublé first because he's a wonderful man. Also, Justin Timberlake, and when I went to see Jay-Z I thought he had amazing stage presence. He could easily stand there and just rap, but he makes everything a show.

What are you listening to right now?
A guy called Passenger, who is really good. I've always listened to Ed Sheeran, and I'm also listening to Skrillex. I've been listening to a lot of Radio One's *Live Lounge* as well.

What's the best gig you've ever been to?
Jay-Z and Kanye West.

LIAM'S PLAYLIST
Haven't Met You Yet – Michael Bublé
Mirrors – Justin Timberlake
Lego House – Ed Sheeran

LOUIS

Who are your biggest musical influences?
Robbie Williams, for his stage presence and natural charisma. I'm always in awe of people like that because I'd love to be that confident on stage.

What are you listening to right now?
Ben Howard, a bit of Green Day, John Mayer, Maroon 5, Passenger and still Ed Sheeran and The Fray.

What's the best gig you've ever been to?
Leeds festival in 2009. Kings of Leon closed it and they were amazing.

LOUIS' PLAYLIST
Angels – Robbie Williams
Only Love – Ben Howard
Let Her Go – Passenger

NIALL

Who are your biggest musical influences?
Bruno Mars, because he's cool, and Michael Bublé because of the way he performs on stage. He's so laid back about it all. He knows how to capture an audience.

What are you listening to right now?
A lot of The Vaccines. We met them when we were in Tokyo. Louis and I went to one of their gigs and I didn't realise how sick they were.

What's the best gig you've ever been to?
I went to a Bon Jovi gig at a stadium in Dublin, which was amazing, and also Jay-Z and Kanye West were unbelievable.

NIALL'S PLAYLIST
Marry You - Bruno Mars
If You Wanna – The Vaccines
Livin' on a Prayer – Bon Jovi

ZAYN

Who are your biggest musical influences?
Justin Timberlake, Michael Jackson, Bob Marley and Usher.

What are you listening to right now?
A lot of rap, like J Cole and Drake. That's the main thing that's on my iPod at the moment.

What's the best gig you've ever been to?
Tinie Tempah at the O2. He was sick.

ZAYN'S PLAYLIST
Thriller – Michael Jackson
Pop Ya Collar – Usher
One Love – Bob Marley

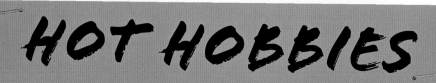

HOT HOBBIES

So, what do the lads get up to on a rare day off?

SURFING
Louis and Liam love tackling the waves. During their recent tour, in the US and Australia the guys headed to the beach whenever they could. The two lads couldn't stop smiling as they took to their surfboards and basked in the sunshine. Liam tweeted, "Me and Louis just went surfing. Louis was up first and for a long one, like 30 FEET!!!! OMG then I stood up on two nice waves woohoo :)"

VINTAGE SHOPPING
Harry is often found in vintage stores trying to find an unusual bargain for his home. He also loves shopping for retro clothes in London's trendy Shoreditch area. Art is a passion and Harry has been spotted at art fairs chatting to up-and-coming artists.

DRAWING
Zayn is pretty talented when it comes to drawing and doodling. He'll often annoy the rest of the band by making them look really ugly in his sketches. "Big cauliflower ears on Niall and a banana on Harry's head," he laughs.

SKATEBOARDING
Zayn is often found speeding down the pavement on top of a sleek skateboard, although it doesn't always end well. "We were in the studio and decided to do a bit of skating," he said. But the floor was a bit slippery and the singer ended up falling off. "The board went over my hand. It hurt so much. I was trying to do a trick and went flying."

SUCH A PERFECT DAY

How would the guys spend their perfect weekend off?

NIALL: I'd wake up at about 10am on Saturday morning, drive to Derby and watch Derby County play with my friends. Then I'd drive back to London and chill out and do nothing. Then maybe I'd go to the pub on the Sunday and have lunch, then do some more lounging.

ZAYN: I'd have absolutely no plans at all. It would just be me, a pair of Nike shorts and my bed. I'd do a lot of sleeping.

LOUIS: I'd lie in until about midday, then watch Jeremy Kyle in bed with a cup of tea. I'd do nothing for the rest of the day, and maybe watch a film on Saturday night. Then I'd play football with my mates on the Sunday.

HARRY: It would involve going to the football with my mates, chilling out a lot and learning the guitar. I'm already learning and I like to get in as much practice as possible.

LIAM: I'd get up out of bed on Saturday and Sunday at about midday. I'd laze around and play *Call of Duty*, then give my mate Andy a call and invite him round. We'd play some more PlayStation™ games and be silly, and maybe go and do some shopping or go to the cinema, then go to a club in the evening.

1D LIFE LESSONS

Try new things
They may be global superstars, but the lads are always keen to try new experiences, whether or not they're good at them. "You have to let yourself do stuff you're not good at," says Liam. Even though we're pretty sure there's not much that One Direction can't do.

Your mum is always right!
All five lads are incredibly close to their mums. Harry says, "Our mums are incredible. They are always there for us." And of course, the 1D mums are rightly proud of their sons. Harry's mum tells him, "You'll always be my little boy."

Keep it real
Despite being the biggest names in music, the guys always keep their feet firmly on the ground. "We don't expect, nor do we want, anyone to treat us differently," says Niall. Just one of the many reasons we love these lads.

The lads have learnt an awful lot on their road to superstardom. Here are their ultimate lessons for life!

Embrace who you are

They may be fully-fledged pop stars, but 1D still have to put up with people saying nasty things about them, just like the rest of us. They don't let other people get them down. "Haters will say what they want, but their hate will never stop you from chasing your dream," says Louis.

Find your own style

One Direction have never been a slave to trends, preferring to wear what they like instead. "Style can be how you carry yourself," Zayn says, "and how you wear whatever you have on." One Direction know the key to looking great is confidence. We couldn't agree more!

"HATERS WILL SAY WHAT THEY WANT, BUT THEIR HATE WILL NEVER STOP YOU FROM CHASING YOUR DREAM."
– LOUIS

TRIVIA QUIZ

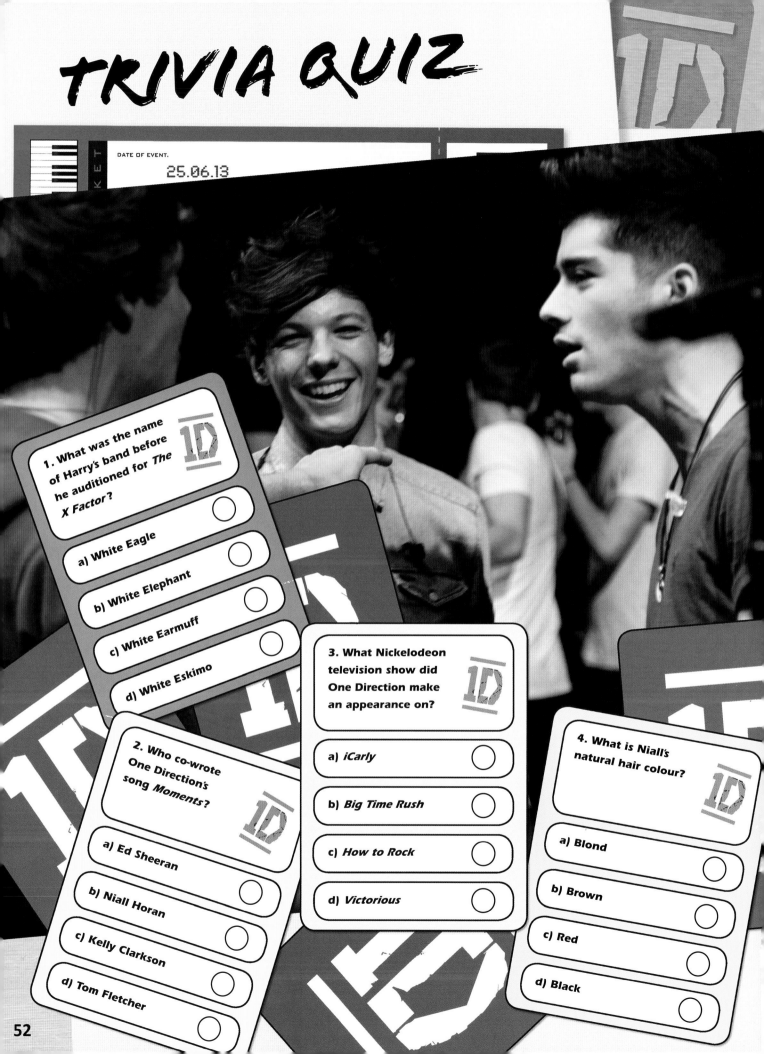

DATE OF EVENT.
25.06.13

1. What was the name of Harry's band before he auditioned for *The X Factor*?

a) White Eagle ◯

b) White Elephant ◯

c) White Earmuff ◯

d) White Eskimo ◯

2. Who co-wrote One Direction's song *Moments*?

a) Ed Sheeran ◯

b) Niall Horan ◯

c) Kelly Clarkson ◯

d) Tom Fletcher ◯

3. What Nickelodeon television show did One Direction make an appearance on?

a) *iCarly* ◯

b) *Big Time Rush* ◯

c) *How to Rock* ◯

d) *Victorious* ◯

4. What is Niall's natural hair colour?

a) Blond ◯

b) Brown ◯

c) Red ◯

d) Black ◯

5. Which guest judge gave Niall the chance to progress on *The X Factor*?

a) Geri Halliwell ◯

b) Katy Perry ◯

c) Pixie Lott ◯

d) Nicole Scherzinger ◯

6. Which song did the band perform at the Olympic Games Closing Ceremony?:

a) *Live While We're Young* ◯

b) *Little Things* ◯

c) *What Makes You Beautiful* ◯

d) *Up All Night* ◯

7. How many songs are there on *Take Me Home: Deluxe Edition*?

a) 15 ◯

b) 17 ◯

c) 18 ◯

d) 16 ◯

8. Which of their music videos was the first to reach 8.24 million views in under 24 hours?

a) *What Makes You Beautiful* ◯

b) *Live While We're Young* ◯

c) *Kiss You* ◯

d) *One Way or Another* ◯

1-3 ADEQUATE ADMIRER

OK, so you didn't get the BEST score, but that doesn't mean you don't still love the lads! Why not have a look at their website and get yourself up to date with all things 1D?

4-6 RIGHT DIRECTION

There's no denying the lads have a special place in your heart, but you're not quite their No.1 fan, yet. Better re-read this annual from front to back, just to make sure!

7-8 SUPER SUPPORTER

Woah. You basically know everything there is to know about 1D – including what they would order at Nandos! You are definitely their biggest fan. Keep up the good work, they love you for it!

ANSWERS
1)b, 2)a, 3)a, 4)b, 5)b, 6)c, 7)b, 8)b

53

ONE DIRECTION LOVE THEIR FANS!

No band has such dedicated fans as One Direction, and Niall, Harry, Zayn, Louis and Liam love them for it...

THERE are no fans as passionate as One Direction fans. They have taken their support and dedication to a level never seen before in pop history. So, it's no wonder the band love their fans so much. The lads know it was their fans who paved the way – getting the word out on Twitter and Tumblr – making One Direction into a worldwide phenomenon. The guys are forever grateful to their fans and are madly in love with them.

"We're massively thankful for all of our fans," says Harry. "We want them to see the real us." The lads always make sure that their Twitter followers are the first to know EVERYTHING they are up to. The guys tweet all of their announcements, from updates on songs to tour news to what they've had for breakfast.

Zayn reckons that One Direction can totally figure out who each fan's favourite member is simply by looking at them. "We all have different sorts of fans," he says. "When they're in the queue, sometimes you can tell who is a fan of who. Just the way they are and

their personalities and stuff, you can kind of tell." Although Harry can't help but joke that's because many fans have the name of their favourite member written on their faces!

One of Harry's favourite memories of a fan encounter was when he was in a sandwich shop and didn't have enough money to pay for his food. "A fan paid for my sandwich," says Harry. "It was so nice."

The guys are given so many gifts by fans, but they try to remember every single one. "I'll never forget the day a fan gave me a lime green monkey," says Zayn. "The gifts we get are interesting!"

One Direction never get tired of fans stopping to talk to them. Incredibly, despite their huge success, they are still honestly shocked when anyone goes out of their way to tell them how much they like their music. "A girl came up to me and said, 'Congratulations on everything you've done,'" Zayn says. "It's really nice when someone says a thing like that. You always remember it."

WE LOVE 1D!

"I love 1D because they are so funny. They support each other and I can't help but smile when I hear their voices!"
HENNIE

"What they do for charity is amazing, I would be the happiest girl alive if I ever met them!"
CHARLOTTE

"They are so inspirational and I love all the songs. They always have fun, mess around and they never fail to make me laugh!"
ELLIE

"I can relate to the songs and their video diaries always make me laugh. There isn't one that I haven't watched! They are just amazing people."
MADELINE

"I love the band for all their different personalities, and how they put smiles on millions of faces. They've changed so many lives in a good way and they never take anything for granted!"
ABIGAIL

1D GIVE BACK

FAME can be a tricky thing. With a vast team of managers, producers, crew and other entourage members surrounding bands, it can be tempting for pop stars to believe the world revolves around them. One Direction are definitely not like that. They've shown time and time again that they are committed to giving back. They give and give and give – not only with money, but also with time. "It's always been incredibly important to us," says Niall. "We know how incredibly lucky we are."

Indeed, One Direction are fast becoming known for the good things they are doing in the world as much as they are for making music. Many celebrities do charity work, but One Direction really stand out. Even when they have a full schedule, they somehow still find the time to give back. And their charitable spirit has caused a whole generation of fans to think about helping others.

Harry, Zayn, Niall, Louis and Liam truly believe that with their celebrity status they can really make a difference in the world and are determined to do just that. "It's such a small thing for us," says Liam. "We love doing things like this. It makes us smile." They are particularly proud of being ambassadors for Rays of Sunshine, which grants the wishes of children with serious or life-limiting illnesses. "It's totally humbling to meet kids like this," says Niall, "and it really makes you feel good that you can do something nice for them."

Not only did the guys record the official Comic Relief single for 2013, they also took a life-changing trip to Ghana to see poverty and slums close up for the first time. The visit turned out to be one of the most amazing and eye-opening experiences of their lives. "I hope we can encourage others to give," says Harry. "I'm just so proud that we were asked to be involved."

When the lads shot their video for *One Way or Another*, it was made up of behind-the-scenes clips of the guys' exciting travels, dancing on their home turf in London, twirling in the middle of Times Square in New York, and laughing with children while volunteering in Ghana. Harry says, "Instead of spending a lot of money on a music video, we decided to make it ourselves while we were on tour and give the money we saved to Comic Relief."

Their Red Nose Day song went on to become the charity's biggest single ever, topping the charts in the UK, the United States and over 60 countries worldwide.

"IT'S TOTALLY HUMBLING TO MEET KIDS LIKE THIS AND IT REALLY MAKES YOU FEEL GOOD THAT YOU CAN DO SOMETHING NICE FOR THEM." – NIALL

1D FUN

Test your brain power with these 1D teasers...

1D WORD PUZZLE
Follow the rules to reveal a 1D message

1. Cross out all the letters in ZAYN
2. Cross out all the remaining letters in HARRY
3. Cross out all 5s, for the number of members in 1D
4. Cross out all 3s, for the place the guys came on *The X Factor*
5. Cross out all 4s, for the number of 1D lads who are from England

```
A Y R Z 1 R 4 A R 3 Y D H R A
5 A R R Y Z 3 3 A N H A L 4 R
Z N A Y O 3 5 Z A Z R N 5 3 4
H Y N 3 N H V 5 3 5 A 3 H N 4
5 H Z Y Z H H Z A E R 5 R 4 Y
Z R 4 Y N 5 A 3 Y 5 4 Z U N !
```

HIGH FIVE

Do you know the answers to these tricky 1D questions?

1. Does NIALL have any brothers or sisters?

2. Where was LOUIS born?

3. What is HARRY's star sign?

4. Which football team does ZAYN support?

5. What is LIAM's middle name? (Hint: it's the same as Niall's!)

GUESS 1D'S HIDDEN TALENTS

Read the clues below, then try to match the boy to the skill

	TALENTS
HARRY Clue: Harry keeps his eye on the ball!	**Rapping**
NIALL Clue: Niall's from Ireland, but he fits in everywhere.	**Skateboarding**
ZAYN Clue: Zayn loves making his own freestyle music.	**Beatboxing**
LIAM Clue: A good beat is all Liam needs to relax!	**Doing accents**
LOUIS Clue: Louis shreds our hearts and the streets.	**Juggling**

THE FUTURE...

ONE Direction's unprecedented rise to fame is matched only by their amazing popularity and awe-inspiring talent. The five lads have a list of achievements that most bands wouldn't hope to attain in their whole career. It's taken a huge amount of hard work, passion and commitment to get where they are, but One Direction are real stars.

From the very beginning they knew what they wanted to accomplish; all they had to do was get everyone else to believe it. As they grow, as they go through more experiences, so their music will continue to develop with them. It's an exciting time,

and of course One Direction have no plans to hold back, they just want to keep growing and achieving.

"We're definitely still learning," says Louis.

"We just want to be the best we can be," says Liam. They're living firmly in the moment and not worrying about what the future holds. "It would be a waste of time to worry about that," says Louis. "At the moment, we're all very happy."

"We know we are living the dream," adds Niall. "I don't know if it will ever sink in."

Stay tuned because their story is bound to get even better...

★ EXCLUSIVE ★

FROM US TO YOU

A special message from the lads

ZAYN: We just want to say thanks, as we always do, because you make the band what it is. Your support and encouragement is always amazing and we're so grateful for everything.

NIALL: I just want to say thank you so much for all of your incredible support over the past few years. The reason we're here today is because of you and we couldn't be more grateful. You're incredible.

LOUIS: I think it's important to let you know that if we're not on Twitter all of the time it doesn't mean we don't care, it just means we're jam-packed with stuff to do. We are incredibly appreciative of your support and we don't want you to think we're ignoring you!

"We love you guys"

LIAM: As always, thank you very much for supporting us. It's been mad and our Twitter followers keep going up and we're selling out tours and it's incredible. None of it would be happening if it wasn't for the fans.

HARRY: Thank you for all your support. We love you guys and you've made all of this happen for us. We appreciate every single little thing you do for us.

"The reason we're here today is because of you"